SO-AOK-488

Cover art by Luke Williams
www.lukelukeluke.com

Branched
© Erin Mallon
Trade Edition, 2016
ISBN 978-1-63092-089-0

NURTURE by Johnna Adams

Synopsis: Doug and Cheryl are horrible single parents drawn together by their equally horrible daughters. The star-crossed parental units' journey from first meeting to first date, to first time, to first joint parent-teacher meeting, to proposal and more. They attempt to form a modern nuclear family while living in perpetual fear of the fruit of their loins and someone abducting young girls in their town.

Cast Size: 1 Male, 1 Female

Branched
a comedy with consequences
by Erin Mallon

Branched had its World Premiere produced by InViolet Theater (co-artistic directors, Angela Razzano and Michael Henry Harris) at HERE Arts Center in New York City on February 20th 2014. The play was directed by Robert Ross Parker with sets and lights by Nick Francone, sound by Shane Rettig, costumes by Kristina Makowski, puppet design and construction by David Valentine, fight choreography by Alexis Black, production management and technical direction by Dylan Luke and stage management by Fran Rubenstein.

The cast was as follows:

Tamara..........................Tara Westwood
Ben...............................Michelle David
Martin............................Andrew Blair
Belinda..........................Marguerite Stimpson

CHARACTERS

TAMARA: (Pronounced TA-mara. Accent on the 1st syllable) 30s, Author, Speaker, Activist, Mother

MARTIN: 42, Manager of an HSBC Bank in Park Slope

BEN: 5 and 1/2, Boy in Belinda's classroom (Ben can be played by any gender).

BELINDA: 30s, Kindergarten teacher at Park Slope Independent Learning School

BEATRICE: Newborn, Ben's little sister. She is "played" by freakish baby doll/puppet creations. She "ages" very quickly throughout and should be "played" by larger, freakier baby doll/puppet creations.

Place: Scene Park Slope, Brooklyn, NY
Time: November into December

BRANCHED

SCENE 1

(November. The first movement of Vivaldi's "Autumn" plays slowly on a violin. Lights up on a modern dining room/kitchen in a Park Slope, New York City apartment. Ben, 5 1/2, stands behind a music stand, practicing his violin while Tamara, 34, places three plates of food down at a beautifully set table. She is hugely pregnant and dressed professionally. Ben wears dress pants and a collared shirt with the top buttons undone. He finishes the piece and looks to Tamara. Silence.)

BEN: Mommy?

TAMARA: Yes angel?

BEN: Was that good?

TAMARA: I don't know Benjamin, was it?

BEN: I think... maybe I played it too adagio?

TAMARA: You sure did. You're getting so good at self-criticism sweetheart! Mommy's so proud of you. See, Vivaldi calls for more of a grandiose style than what you played. What does it say at the top? Certainly not adagio.

BEN: No, certainly not. It says allegro.

TAMARA: Right. Allegro. Do you think you played it allegro?

BEN: No, I think I played it adagio.

TAMARA: You sure did. Good boy. So let me ask you, do you think Mr. Vivaldi up in Heaven feels happy listening to your adagio version of his allegro song?

BEN: No?

TAMARA: That's right. He's doesn't. Remember love, just because some people are dead doesn't mean we can stop respecting them and their music. Should we try it again?

BEN: Yes Mommy, we should.

TAMARA: Terrific. What a determined boy I have.

(Ben launches into his piece in full allegro fashion. Martin, 42, walks in the door, wearing a classy suit.)

BEN: Daddy!!!!!!!!!!!!!!

(Ben puts his violin down, runs and straddle jumps his father.)

MARTIN: Hey Benny Boy! How you doing buddy?

BEN: Great Daddy! I was positive and assertive at school today even in the midst of a conflict!

MARTIN: That's fantastic pal! Proud of you!

BEN: Yes, Daniel Marsh made fun of my suit and I told him he wouldn't be laughing in 30 years when I turn him down for a mortgage!

MARTIN: That's- uh- that's- good, pal.

(Martin and Ben do a lengthy choreographed handshake, which ends in a piggyback ride for Ben. Martin approaches Tamara, Ben still on his back.)

MARTIN: Hi Mommy.

TAMARA: Hi Daddy.

MARTIN: Kiss?

TAMARA: Kiss.

(Martin and Tamara quickly kiss on the lips.)

BEN: *(to Tamara)* Kiss?

TAMARA: Kiss.

(Tamara and Ben quickly kiss on the lips.)

BEN: *(to Martin)* Kiss?

MARTIN: Kiss.

(Martin and Ben quickly kiss on the lips.)

TAMARA: Alright Benjamin. Dismount Daddy so we can disrobe.

(Ben dismounts. All three maintain serious eye contact with one another as they ceremoniously disrobe, revealing Tamara in an elegant slip, and the boys in matching white undershirts, "tightie whitie" briefs, and knee-socks pulled all the way up.)

TAMARA, MARTIN, BEN: *(in unison)* Ahhhhh. Good to be home!

(They quickly and expertly fold their clothes. Tamara suddenly grabs her belly and yells out in pain.)

MARTIN: Tam?

BEN: Mommy, are you ok?

(Beat.)

TAMARA: Mommy's fine. She's just very excited about our bun-less bison burgers. Benjamin, could you be an angel and put our clothes in the family hamper?

BEN: Yes Mommy.

TAMARA: Good boy.

(Ben runs off stage with the clothes.)

MARTIN: Tam? Is it time? Should I blow up the inflatable pool?

TAMARA: Absolutely not. Dinner is on the table. Beatrice can wait until after dessert to be born. *(Tamara grabs a huge pair of earphones and places them around her belly.)* She'll listen to Tony Robbins until we're ready.

(Ben returns.)

TAMARA: Come here angel, it's time for our invocation.

(Tamara and Ben join hands. Martin stares off in the distance.)

TAMARA: Martin!

MARTIN: I'm sorry, what?

TAMARA: I need you awake! *(She snaps.)* Alert! *(She snaps.)* Alive! *(She snaps.)*

MARTIN: Sorry.

(Martin joins hands with them and they all bow their heads. Tamara seizes her stomach again and lets out another painful sound, louder than before. She recovers quickly.)

BEN: Mommy, I'm scared. Hug?

TAMARA: Hug.

(Ben runs to Tamara and hugs her stomach. He is immediately flung across the stage and lands on his bottom.)

BEN: Beatrice kicked me!

TAMARA: *(chiding her stomach)* Beatrice, that's enough. Mommy asked you to be patient and listen to your affirmations. Now apologize to your brother for attacking him.

(Tamara clutches her stomach a third time. She roars in pain while Ben watches from the floor.)

MARTIN: Tamara, I really think I should blow up the pool.

TAMARA: Screw the pool! Get me my birthing stool!

(Martin runs offstage.)

BEN: Mommy?

TAMARA: There's nothing to worry about Ben. Mommy's just going to push a baby out of her nah-nah now. It's all very natural and beautiful. Do you remember what we discussed?

BEN: Yes. "Nah-nahs are channels for children...

BEN AND TAMARA: ...And occasionally portals for pleasure."

TAMARA: That's exactly right. Mommy's nah-nah was born to do this. So now do you think you can serenade Mommy and Daddy while they Hypnobirth your baby sister into the world?

BEN: Yes Mommy, I can.

TAMARA: Such a good boy.

(Ben runs to his violin while Martin returns with the birthing stool. Tamara straddles it. Martin kneels behind her. Ben is ready with his bow. For a moment they are all very still.)

TAMARA: And...Begin.

(Ben slowly plays "Autumn." Martin begins massaging her low back. Tamara breathes slowly and deeply.)

MARTIN: *(in a soothing "hypnosis voice")* "I am fully preparing myself and my baby for a beauuuuutiful, comfortable birthing."

TAMARA: *(in pain, but dealing)* "I am fully preparing myself and my baby for a beauuuuutiful, comfortable birthing." Benjamin sweetie, allegro, remember?

BEN: Oh, yes Mommy. Thank you for your feedback.

(Ben plays quicker. Tamara grabs her belly.)

MARTIN: "I am so relaxed and so safe...."

TAMARA: I AM SO RELAXED AND SO SAFE!!!!! Benjamin darling, where are your dynamics?

BEN: Mommy, I'm allegro-ing as much as I can!

(Tamara grabs her belly again.)

MARTIN: "I am a rainbow... from my pot of gold springs a beauuuuutiful cloud of baby..."

TAMARA: I AM A RAINBOW!!! FROM MY POT OF-BENJAMIN, BRING ME THAT SHEET MUSIC RIGHT NOW!

(Ben stops playing and brings the book over. Tamara grabs it and reads.)

MARTIN: "I am fully preparing myself and my baby for a beauuuuutiful, comfortable birthing."

(For the rest of the scene, Martin repeats the above mantra under Ben and Tamara's lines.)

BEN: Mommy shouldn't you focus on your nah-nah right now?

TAMARA: Mommy's very good at multi-tasking, Ben.

(Beat. Tamara sniffs the air.)

TAMARA: Benjamin, what is that smell on your breath?

BEN: Nothing Mommy.

(Ben backs away.)

TAMARA: Benjamin, you come back to Mommy right now!

(He does.)

TAMARA: Open.

(Ben opens his mouth slightly.)

TAMARA: Wider.

(Ben opens a tiny bit more.)

TAMARA: Benjamin. Did you eat grains?

(Ben shakes his head "no." Tamara pries his mouth open with one hand grasping his upper jaw and the other grasping the lower. Note: this should be weird as hell, but not violent.)

TAMARA: Say "Ah" my love.

(Tamara places her nose into Ben's mouth as she inhales deeply.)

BEN: Ahhhhhhhhhhhhhhhhhhhh.....!

(Tamara is in full labor now and seizes her belly one more time.)

TAMARA: AHHHHHHH.......!!!!!!!!

BEN: Mommy? *(Beat.)* Are these leaves?

MARTIN: Tam? Is everything ok?

(Beat.)

TAMARA: ........AHHHHHHHHHHHHHHHHH!!!!!

BEN: .......AHHHHHHHHHHHHHHHHHH......!!!!

MARTIN: ........AHHHHHHHHHHHHHHHH!!!!!

SCENE 2

(The following morning, 7:20am. Park Slope Independent Learning School. The room is cheerful with children's artwork hanging about on clotheslines. There are various "work stations" along the perimeter, all the proper height for small children to access. Belinda is writing in a festive journal with a girly pen. She is startled by two loud raps on the door. Tamara juts her head into the classroom, her body remaining in the hall.)

TAMARA: Miss Cartwright?

BELINDA: Uh, Belinda, yes. Hi. Ms. Jenkins?

(Belinda's eyes shoot up to her watch.)

TAMARA: Yes, Tamara's fine. I just saw you look at your watch. I realize I am 10 minutes early, but we have a lot to discuss so—

BELINDA: Oh, no, please— I didn't mean to look at the— Please, come in.

(Tamara's body is still partially in the hallway. She speaks to Ben who sits unseen in the hall.)

TAMARA: Now Benjamin, you be good while Mommy speaks with your new teacher. Eh! No. *(covering her breasts with both hands)* Absolutely not. You have ostrich jerky in your pouch if you're hungry and coconut water if you're thirsty. Work on our crossword puzzle. Mommy loves you.

BELINDA: Ms. Jenkins, Benny's welcome to come in and start working if he likes.

15

TAMARA: Thank you Miss Cartwright, but no, "Benny" is not welcome. He'll wait. Kiss kiss, angel.

(Tamara slams the door. She finally enters the room and can be seen in her full glory, perfectly dressed in an egg-plant-colored suit, her hair tied back tightly and elegantly. Her body shows no signs of ever being pregnant. She wears a flesh-tone baby sling strapped across her chest, which carries a baby sleeping, hidden inside. Tamara makes a beeline to Belinda and offers her a firm, quick handshake.)

TAMARA: Thank you for meeting me on such short notice.

BELINDA: Happy to! Would you like to sit down?

(Belinda gestures to a child-size table and chair set. Note: There are no adult-sized chairs in this room. They sit.)

TAMARA: Alright then.

BELINDA: What a beautiful baby! Is she playing with a... stick?

TAMARA: Let's! Get something straight before we begin.

BELINDA: OK.

TAMARA: You are completely taking over for Mrs. Weisenhutter while she's on maternity leave, yes?

BELINDA: *(trying to peek in the sling)* Yes.

TAMARA: So you'll be spending a solid six months in the classroom with my son. Correct?

BELINDA: Correct.

TAMARA: Good. I wouldn't want to spend time building a foundation with you, only to find out you're a
run-of-the-mill substitute teacher who will be out of
here in a few days. I'm sure you understand.

BELINDA: I— think I do.

TAMARA: Terrific. *(She suddenly looks down at her
wristwatch)* Ah. Belinda, pardon us a moment, would
you?

BELINDA: Uh— Sure, sure...

*(Tamara takes a deep breath, closes her eyes and puts her
hands purposefully on the baby.)*

BELINDA: Is everything ok?

TAMARA: Shh!

*(Belinda is silenced. Tamara starts making swirling,
whooshing sounds with her mouth for a good thirty seconds. She finishes. Belinda remains silent.)*

TAMARA: Thank you for that. Today is Beatrice's first
day on the planet. I'm providing womb sounds for her
every hour on the hour so she doesn't feel abandoned
by my body.

BELINDA: Sure, sure.

(Beat. Belinda looks at Tamara's stomach.)

BELINDA: I'm sorry— you gave birth... yesterday?

TAMARA: Last night, you bet.

BELINDA: Wow! But you're so— shouldn't you be resting?

TAMARA: What for? Labor's a breeze if you know how to breathe, and believe me, I do. Do you have children?

BELINDA: No. Not yet, no.

TAMARA: Stay away from women who tell you giving birth is painful. Those women are weak. Here's my advice: have a talk with your uterus now, today, before you even conceive. Unless of course you are pregnant already. Are you? Are you pregnant?

BELINDA: No, I'm not.

TAMARA: Terrific. Here's what you do then. Tell your uterus that you are the boss. You decide when the contractions come and how long they last. You create your birth story. You are the dominatrix of your birth canal.

(Beat.)

BELINDA: Oh! Now? Talk to it now?

TAMARA: No time like the present.

BELINDA: Um. I— think we'll chat later. If you don't mind.

TAMARA: Why would I mind? You are entitled to make your own decisions, however misguided. I've only written a slew of books on feminine energy, natural birthing, and proper parenting. Surely I don't know what I'm talking about.

BELINDA: *(pronouncing her name taMAra)* No, I'm certain you do! I just— forgive me Tamara, I didn't mean to offend.

TAMARA: You're forgiven. Alright, enough of that! Let's—

BELINDA: Gosh, I'm sorry to interrupt you— I'm working on not doing that— but... *(looking her up and down)* I'm just so distracted by your... *(looks down and considers)*

TAMARA: Physique?

BELINDA: Well, yes! How did you...?

TAMARA: Easily. I went to the gym this morning and everything went right back into place. Being slim is a decision. You either make it or you don't.

BELINDA: Tell that to my thighs!

TAMARA: Gladly. Swing them this way please.

(Beat.)

BELINDA: Oh. I was just— joking actually. I don't need you to tell them anything.

TAMARA: Fair enough. Although I wouldn't joke about my thighs if I were you, Belinda. *(quick beat)* Alright, you've gotten us off-track. We are not here to talk to your thighs...

BELINDA: No, we're not.

TAMARA: ...nor are we here to chat with your uterus.

BELINDA: Certainly not.

TAMARA: I'm sure you are well aware of why I'm here.

BELINDA: Actually... no. I'm not.

TAMARA: No?

BELINDA: No.

(Beat.)

TAMARA: No idea.

BELINDA: No.

TAMARA: Fascinating.

(Beat.)

BELINDA: *(pronouncing her name taMAra again)* Um. Tamara, you should know that Ben is really doing beautifully. Even after just one day with him, I can tell how bright he is— and funny! So funny! Oh gosh, you have to hear this— listen to this— he comes up to me yesterday and says—

TAMARA: Don't bother. I can hear his witticisms at home. I'm here because of the Cheerios incident.

(Beat.)

BELINDA: The "Cheerios Incident".

TAMARA: Indeed.

BELINDA: *(pronouncing it wrong a third time)* Forgive me Tamara, but I don't know what "incident" you're talking about.

TAMARA: It's TAmara, not taMAra. The accent is on the first syllable, not the second.

BELINDA: Oh. I'm sorry. *(trying it out and failing)* TAM-ra.

TAMARA: Let's just stick with Ms. Jenkins.

BELINDA: Great.

TAMARA: Great. Now, since you don't seem to know what goes on in your classroom, let me fill you in.

(Beat.)

TAMARA: *(getting a little choked up)* I'm sorry. This is difficult for me.

BELINDA: Oh my goodness, what is it?

TAMARA: Benjamin came home last night with— Cheerios on his breath. It seems that little Jeremiah Parker boy took it upon himself to share his snack with my son.

BELINDA: Ok...

(Beat.)

BELINDA: I'm sorry, is that the problem?

TAMARA: You allow snack sharing?

BELINDA: Sure. We encourage it!

TAMARA: He gave him Cheerios, Miss Cartwright! With MILK! Is that something you encourage?

BELINDA: Well, I don't know. Ben doesn't have any food allergies, does he? I checked!

TAMARA: Benjamin, I'll have you know, is a strict follower of the Paleo Diet.

BELINDA: The Paleo Diet?

TAMARA: Yes! No carbs, no dairy, and no grains of any kind. If Benjamin can't pick it from the ground or chase it and kill it, then he should not be eating it.

BELINDA: Tama- Ms. Jenkins, I apologize for the oversight, truly. We pay great attention to what the kids are eating, but when it comes to these fad diets—

TAMARA: Whoa, whoa whoa. Fad diet, did you say?

BELINDA: Poor choice of words. It's just— I am Ben's kindergarten teacher, not his personal trainer and— Oh god, that sounded ruder than I intended. Not that I intended to be—

(Beat. She breathes.)

BELINDA: Actually, yes! This may make you feel better! I know for a fact that Jeremiah's mother packs him "Oat-holes." They are a *(singing a little commercial ditty)* "Sugar free, healthy alternative to Cheerios!

Bing!" No big deal, right? Ben had a little snack, made a new friend, and certainly did not die.

(Beat.)

BELINDA: Right?

(Tamara covers the baby's ears.)

TAMARA: You're damn right he did not die! No thanks to you! Thank God he had the good sense to confess so we could get them out of his system immediately!

BELINDA: Immediately? You mean— I'm sorry, what do you mean?

TAMARA: We threw up those Oat-holes.

(Beat.)

BELINDA: Wait— you made your son throw up?

TAMARA: No, I did not make him throw up. He chose to throw up. We did it together. I lent him my support.

BELINDA: You and your five-year-old purposely vomited together.

TAMARA: You bet we did. And we would do it again.

(Beat.)

TAMARA: Belinda, how many stomachs do you have?

BELINDA: How many...

TAMARA: ...stomachs do you have?

BELINDA: Uh... one.

TAMARA: Correct. One. And how many does a cow have?

(Tamara pulls a cow puppet out of her bag and places it on Belinda's hand. Beat.)

BELINDA: Four?

TAMARA: Gold star. Four. Now, how many breasts do I have?

(Tamara pulls out two squeezy stress balls that look like squeezy breasts. Note: these exist. They're fantastic)

TAMARA: Go on.

BELINDA: You have two breasts. Ms. Jenkins, this is—

TAMARA: Excellent. Now describe to me how a cow's udders differ in appearance from a woman's breasts.

BELINDA: Ms. Jenkins, this is starting to get offensive.

TAMARA: It certainly is. Congratulations, that is the first intelligent thing you've said today! Moral of the story: cows and humans are different. Now, how "offended" would you be if I stuck my breast into your cow's mouth?

(Tamara places her stress ball in the cow puppet's mouth.)

TAMARA: You'd be VERY offended. Not only would your cow be confused and emotionally damaged, but he would get sick. Terribly, physically sick. His four stomachs cannot tolerate the milk from my two breasts. It's not meant for him. *(Beat.)* When you expose my child to "Oat-Holes" and bovine milk, that's exactly what you are doing. You are shoving your cow udders into my human baby's mouth and I will not sit idly by and watch that happen.

(Tamara has the cow puppet's udders dangerously close to Belinda's mouth. A long silence. Tamara breaks their face-off, tears the puppet off Belinda's hand and places her props back in her bag.)

TAMARA: *(suddenly cheery)* I trust that we have learned something here today, and there will be no further incidents of this nature.

(Beat.)

TAMARA: A pleasure to meet you. Your skirt is just darling.

(Tamara exits. Belinda is left alone and bewildered.)

SCENE 3

(Later that same day. A practically empty living room. Two bowls of ice cream are placed on the coffee table, along with whipped cream, chocolate sauce and cherries. Belinda wears an ill-fitting "business" blazer. She's gripping a baseball bat, ready to attack.)

BELINDA Yes?

MARTIN: *(from offstage)* Hi! I'm here to look at the apartment?

BELINDA: Your name?

MARTIN: It's Martin? We spoke on the phone?

BELINDA: Can you prove that?

MARTIN: I'm sorry?

BELINDA: Can you prove that we spoke on the phone and you are who you say you are?

MARTIN: Oh yes! The uh— the secret word is— "platypus"?

(Belinda drops the bat and lets Martin in.)

BELINDA: *(cheery)* Hi! Apologies for the terrible customer service you just received there. I'm new to this real estate adventure and I'm still experimenting with how not to get raped and pillaged whilst on the job.

(Beat.)

BELINDA: I watched "The Accused" recently.

MARTIN: O-K?

BELINDA: Jodie Foster film? 1988? Let's start from scratch. *(extending her hand)* Belinda Cartwright, real estate agent.

MARTIN: Martin Laurence, banker.

BELINDA: Martin Lawrence?

(Beat.)

BELINDA: As in "Bad Boys", "Blue Streak", "Talkin Dirty After Dark...?"

MARTIN: Yes, sounds alike but spelled differently. His Lawrence is spelled with a "W", mine has a "U" like Laurence Olivier.

BELINDA: Oh. I can tell by the way you had that little speech prepared that people do that to you all the time, don't they?

MARTIN: It does come up. Not to worry though—

BELINDA: No. That's a very annoying thing to do to a person. You, Martin Laurence, should be able to say your own beautiful name out loud without me listing the titles of violent films you did not star in.

MARTIN: Thank you.

(Beat.)

MARTIN: So. Can I... have a look?

BELINDA: *(confused)* Um. Sure— Uh...

(Belinda spins around awkwardly, thinking he wants to "have a look" at her. Beat.)

MARTIN: I meant the apartment, but... you look lovely.

BELINDA: Oh gosh, of course! Forgive me, I didn't mean to wrestle that compliment out of you.

MARTIN: Not a problem. Freely given.

BELINDA: *(dropping into a seductive voice)* So... Wrestling, huh?

MARTIN What?

BELINDA: *("normal" voice)* Your body looks strong, like you maybe wrestled in high school?

MARTIN: No no. Never wrestled. Do you... mind if I—?

BELINDA: *(gesturing to the apartment)* Please, look, look!

(Martin walks past her and begins looking around. Belinda whips her head left and right. She shakes her suit, trying to smell it.)

BELINDA: Ohmygod what is that?

MARTIN: Pardon?

BELINDA: Do I smell?!!

(Martin sniffs the air.)

MARTIN: I don't think so? I mean, not that I can tell.

(Belinda flops down on the couch, relieved.)

BELINDA: Oh god, sorry! You know when you catch a whiff of something... pungent, and you're instantly terrified it's you?

MARTIN: Sure, sure.

(Beat.)

MARTIN: Is it— me?

BELINDA: Of course not! *(seductive voice)* Someone as attractive as you couldn't possibly smell.

(Beat. Martin can't help laughing.)

BELINDA: *(normal voice)* It's official, I've decided to plan all my sentences in my head before I dare let them out into the world. Who cares if there are inappropriately long pauses in my conversations? At least I won't live in a constant state of regret.

MARTIN: No, no. It was a compliment. *(quick beat)* I liked it.

BELINDA: *(seductive voice)* And you didn't even have to wrestle me for it.

(Beat.)

29

BELINDA: *(normal voice)* So! How can I service you here today Martin Laurence? Wait, before you answer! Full disclosure? We have ourselves an absolute first-timer here. Passed the real-estate exam through some act of god or computer malfunction, because seriously? NO clue what I'm doing.

MARTIN: Alright then.

BELINDA: Times are hard. Gal has to juggle a few professions.

MARTIN: Sure, sure.

(She mimes juggling.)

BELINDA: Yeah, got lots of ball-jobs up in the air.

MARTIN: Huh?

BELINDA: Just— you've been warned.

MARTIN: Fair enough.

(Beat.)

BELINDA: Please. Continue.

MARTIN: Alright. Well, I'm considering— and only considering at this point— certainly not ready to put down a payment or anything… A change.

BELINDA: Well don't.

MARTIN: I'm sorry?

BELINDA: Don't you dare change, you! I was just thinking how fantastic you look in that suit. *(singing)*
"Don't go changin' to try and please me...."

(Beat.)

BELINDA: *(spoken)* "Just the Way You Are"? Billy
Joel? The Stranger album!!!!

MARTIN: No no, I'm familiar with the song, I just—

BELINDA: Oh good. I was gonna say!!!

MARTIN: I was just talking about a change in my - my
uh – my living situation. I guess you'd say.

BELINDA: Oh, say no more! Roommates?

MARTIN: *(quick beat)* Sort of.

BELINDA: Roommates suck! As does the awkward way
you're standing up while I'm sitting down. Come. Sit
beside me. Have a sundae.

(Beat. Martin stays standing.)

BELINDA: I prepared rapidly melting ice cream sundaes
in honor of my first "client."

(Beat. Martin doesn't move.)

BELINDA: Too much?

MARTIN: No, it's just— I don't normally ingest lactose,
so—

BELINDA: Oh! Well then today's your lucky day Martin Laurence! I didn't put an ounce of lactose on this ice cream! So you'll be just fine.

(Martin laughs.)

MARTIN: Then I guess... I guess... I'll be fine then.

(He sits on the couch, a cushion of distance between them. Belinda picks up a spoonful of ice cream and raises it in his direction.)

BELINDA: Cheers.

(Martin lifts his spoon.)

MARTIN: Cheers.

(They clink. Belinda watches Martin as he eats. It's clear it's been a very looooong time since he's had ice cream.)

MARTIN: Mmmmmmmmmmmm.

BELINDA: Mmmmmmmmmmmm. Good, huh?

MARTIN: Mmmmmmmmmmm-Hmmmmmmmmmm.

BELINDA: *(seductive voice)* Yes, Mmmmmmmmmmmm. I wasn't sure which... condom-ints... you preferred though.

MARTIN: What?

BELINDA: *(back to "regular" voice)* Feel free to throw some cherries and chocolate sauce and such on your ice cream.

MARTIN: Oh, great. Thank you.

(Martin piles on the condiments.)

BELINDA: So. How many roommates you got?

MARTIN: *(while he eats)* Uh... two. Well, no. I guess it's two and... a half now? She's new. The half, I mean. No. I'm sorry. She's not a half, she's a whole, she's a person. So yes, she is definitely whole.

(Beat. Belinda is confused. Martin looks up.)

MARTIN: Three. I have three roommates.

BELINDA: Gotcha. Three's a lot! I lived with three girls from college once. Did not go well, so I feel your pain.

MARTIN: Well, it did go well. In the beginning. *(quick beat)* Wait.

BELINDA: What?

MARTIN: Did it?

BELINDA: Did what?

MARTIN: Did it ever go well?

BELINDA: I don't know, I don't know these people.

MARTIN: No, I'm asking myself.

BELINDA: Oh. *(quick beat)* Well did it?

MARTIN: Maybe it didn't.

BELINDA: Huh.

(Beat. Martin is lost.)

BELINDA: Well, it sounds like maybe you should get the hell outta there! Being alone is fantastic — or so I tell myself on the rare occasion when I'm not crying. Seriously though, I do everything alone! Eat! Bathe! Watch "Hoarders!" Everything. It's great!

MARTIN: No no, I can't — just leave.

BELINDA: Why not?

MARTIN: My uh... My — younger roommate. He's.... Well, he's amazing. Gosh, I used to hate when people said the whole "You won't understand love until you have..." roommates — thing. But, they were right! I didn't understand. Now though. Now — I want him to proud of me, ya know? I want him to really know me. And — if I only saw him on weekends? I don't know if— No. No, I couldn't do that. No.

(Beat.)

BELINDA: You're such a tender and devoted roommate.

MARTIN: Thanks.

BELINDA: I like that.

(Belinda makes a quick move and slides next to Martin, pushing her nose into his neck. She inhales deeply. Beat. Martin is frozen.)

BELINDA: Oh, that smell is you.

MARTIN: *(startled)* It is?!?

BELINDA: *(still smelling his neck)* Yeah, but it's not —
bad. It's just... spicy?

MARTIN: I wear old spice cologne.

BELINDA: Mmmm. So does my Dad.

(Belinda slides her nose upward to reach his cheek.)

BELINDA: Ohhhhhhhh. Now that I like.

MARTIN: What's that? What-what-what what do you
like?

BELINDA: I'll admit it, your neck-smell had me feeling
conflicted a moment ago, but your face?? Your face-
smell is delicious! Like gum. Or clean teeth.

MARTIN: I wash with peppermint soap.

BELINDA: You have such a festive hygiene routine,
Martin Laurence!

MARTIN: Thank you.

*(Belinda pulls back a few inches and looks him deeply in
the eyes.)*

BELINDA: No, thank you.

(Beat.)

MARTIN: Um. I think I need some whipped cream.

BELINDA: Go right ahead.

(Martin grabs the bottle of whipped cream.)

BELINDA: Martin?

MARTIN: Yes?

BELINDA: *(seductive voice)* This has been really great. But you didn't come here for an ice cream social, did you. You came to see some real estate. And I'm the agent that's going to show it to you. Let's start with the basement.

(She moves his hand between her legs.)

BELINDA: Shall we?

MARTIN: Um.

(Martin shoots his whipped cream into the air.)

SCENE 4

(Tamara and Ben stand "disrobed" in the living room, holding hands. Beatrice is still strapped to Tamara, only this time she is "awake." She is a frightening baby with shocking red hair, and beady eyes which never blink. Instead of arms and legs, Beatrice has four branches sticking out from her hard little torso. Perhaps some dark berries or leaves grow on them. Tamara and Ben stare at the door in silence. Martin rushes in, completely out of breath. Beat.)

BEN: Hi Daddy.

MARTIN: Hi Bud. *(quick beat)* Hi Mommy.

(Beat.)

TAMARA: Hello Daddy.

BEN: *(to Martin)* Kiss?

MARTIN: Kiss.

(Ben and Martin quickly kiss.)

BEN: *(to Tamara)* Kiss?

TAMARA: Kiss.

(Ben and Tamara quickly kiss.)

MARTIN: Sorry I'm late Tam. Kiss?

(Beat. She makes him wait.)

TAMARA: Kiss.

(Martin attempts a longer-than-usual kiss.)

TAMARA: Oh my lord, did you ingest lactose?

MARTIN: No! Of course not.

(Martin crouches down to see Bea. It's clear he has a hard time looking directly at her.)

MARTIN: Well, look who's... up! Hey there Bea! How's Daddy's... little girl?

BEN: *(loudly)* Yeah, hi Bea! How's... brother's... little sister?

(Tamara covers the baby's ears.)

TAMARA: Martin and Benjamin, that is much too loud! This is her first day outside the womb!

MARTIN: Sorry Mommy.

BEN: Sorry Mommy.

(Beat.)

TAMARA: It's OK boys. She's just used to my amniotic fluids softening the sounds she hears, so you'll both need to be more gentle with your decibels.

MARTIN: Right. Of course.

TAMARA: We were about to start dinner without you. Where were you?

MARTIN: I'm sorry, I should have called. I had a last minute meeting I had to take as the bank was closing.

TAMARA: Alright, well can we start our meal now please? It's past 6 o'clock.

MARTIN: Absolutely. There's nothing I'd like more.

(Martin sits down at the table. Ben follows suit.)

TAMARA: Excuse me gentlemen! Is this a world where we eat before connecting and invoking?

BEN: No Mommy it's not.

MARTIN: No Mommy it's not. Sorry Tam.

(Martin quickly strips down to his underwear and folds his clothes. Ben runs his clothes to the family hamper.)

TAMARA: What's come over you today? You're late, you smell like a cow teat, and now you're running to your food, fully-clothed like an animal at the trough?

MARTIN: I suppose I am just... going-with-the-flow today.

TAMARA: Well please don't.

MARTIN: Alright I won't.

TAMARA: Good. Let's join hands.

(Ben returns. All three join hands, bow their heads, and speak in unison.)

TAMARA, MARTIN, BEN: Dear Universal Energy, we invoke you now to bless this food. May it nourish our very attractive bodies. May you always guide us as your stewards of magnificence on this planet. And may our subordinates stand forever in awe of us, quaking in fear of us when it is appropriate. We are powerful, we are delightful, we are the Jenkins-Laurence Family. Amen.

(They sit. Tamara moves the baby to her breast. Everyone begins eating. Tamara winces.)

BEN: Mommy, does that hurt?

TAMARA: Yes. At first it does hurt Ben. But after a moment it's actually quite... pleasurable.

BEN: Mommy?

TAMARA: Yes Ben.

BEN: Why didn't Bea do the invocation with us?

TAMARA: Your sister is still very little sweetheart, so she can't talk yet. Until she learns to verbalize, we all have to be very sensitive to her signals. Did you see how just a moment ago, I moved Beatrice to my boobie?

BEN: Yes, I did.

TAMARA: I could tell by her squirming that she was hungry and needed Mommy's milk.

BEN: I didn't see her squirm.

TAMARA: *(an outsized reaction)* WELL SHE DID!!!!

(They continue to eat. Ben starts to squirm.)

BEN: I'm squirming too Mommy. Can I have some of your milk for dessert?

TAMARA: No Benjamin, you'll be having poached pears for dessert. You drank from Mommy's boobies for almost five whole years. It's Bea's turn. You're a big boy now, and...?

BEN AND TAMARA: "Big boys don't need boobies."

TAMARA: That's exactly right. Drink your lemon water.

(They eat in silence.)

BEN: Mommy?

TAMARA: Yes angel.

BEN: Why does Baby Bea have sticks where arms and legs are supposed to be?

(Tamara slams down her fork.)

TAMARA: *(trying to stay composed)* Benjamin, you can ask me that question a million times and the answer will still be the same. Your sister is...

BEN: "a creative soul who marches to her own drummer. We support her unique appearance no matter how humiliating it is for us as a family."

TAMARA: Good boy. *(to Martin)* Sweetheart, how are the Portobello pods?

MARTIN: Outstanding.

TAMARA: I'm glad you like them. Things go well at the bank today?

MARTIN: They did. How was your day sweetness?

BEN: Mommy yelled at my new teacher.

MARTIN: She did? You did?

TAMARA: Benjamin, were you eavesdropping on Mommy's grown-up conversation?

BEN: No. Yes. Oops.

MARTIN: Was everything alright at school, Tam?

TAMARA: Fine. I did not yell at your teacher, Benjamin. I simply yet aggressively informed her of the way we deserve to be treated. Remember sweetheart, most people aren't as smart as we are, so we need to teach them how to behave, even if that means losing some friends. Mommy doesn't have any friends. And Mommy doesn't care.

BEN: I'll be your friend Mommy.

TAMARA: You're my son, silly. We can't be friends.

MARTIN: So Benny boy, tell me about your new teacher. Is she nice?

BEN: Oh yes, she's nice and pretty and-

TAMARA: Meek. I have no tolerance for women like that.

MARTIN: No, you don't.

TAMARA: Nor should I!

MARTIN: No, nor should you! I agree!

TAMARA: Beatrice, are you squirming again?

(Tamara moves Beatrice to the other breast and is in obvious agony. Ben starts squirming again.)

TAMARA: Benjamin?

(He stops.)

TAMARA: Benjamin, could you please consult Calvin and tell us what our family can look forward to these next few days?

BEN: Of course Mommy!

(Ben runs up to the family planner which hangs on the wall.)

BEN: Calvin the Calendar says tonight is Educational Game Night, so we will be playing "Trivial Pursuit: Book Lover's Edition" after we eat. Oh I hope we touch on Charles Dickens, I really do.

TAMARA: Me too Ben. Stories of orphans are always good for lifting the spirit and making one grateful.

BEN: Ooh! And tomorrow night is Classical Music Night! Mommy will lead us in a dinner discussion on Tchaikovsky and his contributions to the Romantic Era, followed by a brief violin concert in the living room performed by me, Ben.

MARTIN: You'll do great Buddy.

BEN: And speaking of the Romantic Era, Saturday of course is Mommy and Daddy's "Sex and Recreation Day", so I will be visiting with Grandma.

TAMARA: Yes you will. Come finish your pods, Ben. Excellent job with Calvin. Mommy and Daddy are looking forward to their special time together Saturday, aren't they Daddy?

MARTIN: They sure are. It's been a long week.

TAMARA: Though we will miss you very much angel. Won't we Daddy?

(Martin leans over and kisses Ben's head.)

MARTIN: You betcha kiddo. You're our best boy.

(Tamara kisses Baby Bea's head.)

TAMARA: And you're our best girl Beatrice. We are so very lucky, aren't we Daddy?

(Beat.)

TAMARA: Aren't we Daddy?

MARTIN: Oh! Yes we are sweetheart. We are very lucky indeed.

SCENE 5

(Friday morning, 7:45am. Martin and Ben walk into Belinda's classroom wearing suits and carrying briefcases.)

BELINDA: Martin?

MARTIN: Belinda? What the hell are you doing here?

BEN: Daddy, you said hell!

MARTIN: I know, I'm sorry pal — I'm dropping my kid off at— Did you— follow me here?

BELINDA: No, I'm—

MARTIN: How did you know I—?

BELINDA: I didn't! Why didn't you tell me you were—?

MARTIN: I didn't know that you taught at—

BELINDA: Well I didn't know you were Ben's—

MARTIN: But you said you were in real estate! You—

BELINDA: I am! Times are hard, remember? A gal has to—

MARTIN: "Juggle several—"

BEN: Daddy?

(Silence.)

BEN: Have you met my new teacher before?

(Martin and Belinda over-lap)

MARTIN: Uh, sort of buddy, I—

BELINDA: Yes Ben, you see we—

(Beat.)

BEN: Daddy. Belinda. Use your words.

MARTIN: That's a great idea Ben. Let's use our words. Yesterday, Daddy was...

BELINDA: ...looking for a new apartment for you! Isn't that exciting?

MARTIN: No no Ben, that's not exactly—

BEN: Oh that is exciting!

BELINDA: And I was the completely platonic real estate agent who serviced him!

BEN: Oh wow! We're moving!

MARTIN: Benny, we're not moving, Daddy was just—

BEN: Do I get my own room? Sharing with Bea is scary.

MARTIN: Benjamin let's calm down now—

BELINDA: Oh. Wait. I'm confused now. Should I not have said anything about—

BEN: Belinda, I had no idea you were in real estate!

BELINDA: I am, Ben. See, I'm what you'd call a "Jack of all Trades, Master of Nothing."

BEN: I'd be careful with that if I were you, Belinda. Mommy says you have to pick a "major" in life very early on or else you're destined to be a drain on society.

MARTIN: Ben, that's enough!!! Listen buddy, I know you like to talk business—

BEN: I really do. *(to Belinda)* My major is business.

MARTIN: —But, Daddy needs to speak privately with your teacher now, alright? And we are not moving.

BEN: Awwwww!

MARTIN: Everything is staying the same. This was all just a silly misunderstanding.

BEN: But—

MARTIN: Ben?

BEN: Al-right. *(to Belinda)* If it's all the same to you, I'd like to get my work started early today, before my inferior classmates arrive and inevitably impede my learning.

BELINDA: Sure, Ben. That's fine.

(Ben jogs across the classroom, throws a "work mat" down on the floor, dumps out some blocks and starts building with gusto. Belinda and Martin are left standing in silence.)

BELINDA: So.

MARTIN: Yes.

(Beat.)

BELINDA: Your very special roommate is Ben!

MARTIN: Yes. Ben.

BELINDA: Great kid.

MARTIN: He is.

(Beat.)

BELINDA: And... your other roommate is?

MARTIN: Tamara. My wife.

BELINDA: Right. Yes. I met her! She's... a sweetie.

MARTIN: Well.

BELINDA: And, um... I'm sorry — just playing a little catch-up here—

MARTIN: Sure, sure.

BELINDA: The "half" roommate? Who is that?

MARTIN: Our daughter.

BELINDA: Right. The baby!

MARTIN: I shouldn't have called her that. She just— has some problems. I guess I don't yet know how to... *(Beat.)* Anyway. *(Beat.)*

BELINDA: Hey, um. I sorta wish you told me you were married.

MARTIN: We didn't do anything wrong though! I stopped it before we could!

BELINDA: Sure, but remember the part before you stopped it? The part where I used my "sexy voice," ran my nose up the side of your face and put your hand on my "basement"?

MARTIN: Yes. Yes, I do remember that. I'm sorry Belinda. My life is hitting a bit of a rough patch right now. To be honest, I don't know what the hell I'm doing.

BELINDA: No no, I'm sure this is my fault somehow! I'm a terrible read of human beings. I mean, I just assumed you were interested since you let me—

BEN: A-S-S-U-M-E makes an ass of you and me!!!!

MARTIN: Ben? What's that you're making over there, a barn?

BEN: It's the New York Stock Exchange.

MARTIN: Terrific. Stay focused buddy. *(Beat.)* OK. I should probably just — go. I'm truly sorry.

BELINDA: OK.

MARTIN: OK.

(Beat. Martin doesn't move. He stares at Belinda.)

MARTIN: OK.

(Martin bolts across the room to Ben and kisses him on the head)

MARTIN: Keep up the good work kiddo. Love you big guy.

(Ben pulls Martin down so he can kiss his head.)

BEN: Love you too, big guy!

(Martin exits, then immediately pops his head back in.)

MARTIN: *(whispering to Belinda)* So, I'll see you tomorrow night then, right?

BELINDA: *(whispering)* Wait. What?

MARTIN: *(whispering)* Well, when I left last night you invited me to another "open house" tomorrow.

BELINDA: *(whispering)* Right, I did, but I figured that was off now.

MARTIN: *(whispering)* Why?

BELINDA: *(whispering)* Oh, see, when I said "open house" I was actually using that as a metaphor for sexual intercourse.

MARTIN: *(whispering)* Sure, I picked up on the metaphor—

BELINDA: *(whispering)* Oh good. For a second there I was worried I was too subtle.

MARTIN: *(whispering)* There's nothing subtle about you Belinda.

BELINDA: *(whispering)* Good to know. But, see, the thing is, you're married. So I'm guessing you can get all your sexual intercourse at home, right?

MARTIN: *(whispering)* Right. I can, but— I mean— I— I just really enjoyed spending time with you, even without the-the-the—

BELINDA: *(whispering)* Intercourse. Right. I know. Me too.

MARTIN: *(whispering)* And I'd really like to see you again. Listen. Ben's mom and I schedule time on Saturday evenings to do our own separate activities, so it's kind of perfect.

BELINDA: *(whispering)* Perfect for what though? What kind of activities will we be doing?

MARTIN: *(whispering)* I'm not sure.

BELINDA: *(whispering)* Sexual activities?

(Ben has tip-toed to the door, unnoticed by the adults.)

MARTIN: *(whispering)* I'm... not sure Belinda. We'll figure it out tomorrow, ok?

BEN: *(whispering)* Daddy, isn't tomorrow Mommy Daddy Sex Day?

BELINDA: *(whispering)* What did he say? What did you say?

BEN: *(whispering)* I said—

MARTIN: *(full voice)* Nothing! Stay focused big guy! Daddy loves you!

(Martin slams the door. Belinda and Ben are left looking at one another. Belinda smiles. Ben smiles.)

SCENE 6

(Saturday, 3pm. Tamara and Martin's living room. Sounds of passionate kissing. Martin is on his knees, facing the couch, his back to the audience, hiding Tamara from view.)

MARTIN: My wife is so sexy.

TAMARA: Yes she is.

MARTIN: I'm so damn lucky.

TAMARA: Yes you are.

MARTIN: I love you so much.

TAMARA: Yes you do.

(Tamara abruptly stops kissing him.)

TAMARA: Hold on one second.

(She heaves her body to one side of the couch. We now see that she is still wearing Beatrice strapped to her. Beat.)

TAMARA: Oy.

MARTIN: What's wrong?

TAMARA: I'm usually much more aroused by you than I am today.

MARTIN: Oh yeah?

TAMARA: Mm-hmm.

MARTIN: Hm.

(They sit by side and think a moment.)

MARTIN: Do you think perhaps having Beatrice here is killing the mood?

(Tamara covers the baby's ears.)

TAMARA: Martin! What an awful thing to say. She can hear you!

MARTIN: She can also see us, Tam. I just think, maybe this is — potentially... damaging to her?

TAMARA: Martin, she was created through our love-making, so surely she can...

MARTIN AND TAMARA: ...be a witness to our love-making.

MARTIN: Yeah, I get that. I just don't know if I agree with it.

TAMARA: It worked fine for Benjamin!

MARTIN: Did it?

TAMARA: Martin, sex has been scheduled so sex needs to be had. And leaving Beatrice without nurturing touch is not an option.

MARTIN: Fair enough.

TAMARA: Plus I could really use the sex this afternoon. It would be a wonderful warm-up for my speech tonight. By the way, what will you be doing for your Saturday Night Solo Activity?

MARTIN: Just... reading. Boring stuff really.

TAMARA: Oh good. Yes, sex really liberates my vocal chords. And a person who's just had sex gives off a terrifically confident glow. Very good for book sales. Alright, let's get back on track.

MARTIN: Let's.

TAMARA: I really want this to be successful sex for both of us.

MARTIN: As do I.

TAMARA: Fantastic. Same page. Sex is very important.

MARTIN: Without a doubt.

TAMARA: One must be creative about it.

MARTIN: One must. *(Beat.)* Do we need our song then?

TAMARA: We do.

(Martin walks over to the stereo and pauses.)

MARTIN: *(looking at Beatrice)* Just— watch the sticks, please.

(Martin switches on some music. A hardcore rap song with a good dance beat. Mystikal's "Shake it Fast" would work nicely. Tamara is visibly and instantly turned on.

She stands up and starts to dance a little. She gestures to "turn up the music." He does. She gestures again. He turns it up more. She gestures once more. Now it's very loud. Martin and Tamara must shout over the music.)

MARTIN: How's that?!

TAMARA: Oh that's wonderful! I love the way he raps out orders! It's so!- so!- ...virile!

(Tamara closes her eyes and continues to dance.)

MARTIN: Mommy likes this song, doesn't she!

TAMARA: She does! She does!

MARTIN: Mommy's letting her hair down!

TAMARA: She is! She is!

MARTIN: Mommy likes Sexy Saturday, doesn't she!

TAMARA: Yes she doooooooooeeeeessss!

(The music continues to blast as Tamara runs and leaps on Martin, almost knocking him over. He catches her. They kiss. It's violent. He puts her down suddenly. She looks surprised to be on her feet. This isn't part of the choreography! Martin shuts off the music.)

MARTIN: *(re: Beatrice)* Is she ok?

TAMARA: *(looking down quickly)* Yes. Beatrice is a tough little girl. I'm so proud of her.

MARTIN: Ok good. Me too.

(Martin switches the music back on. Tamara pushes him. He doesn't push back. She slaps him. He doesn't slap back. He comes in for another kiss. She responds. Again, it's violent, but no one's complaining. They make their way down to the floor. They roll in one direction. Then they roll in the other, a family love-sandwich. Tamara suddenly springs to her feet and slaps off the music, leaving Martin on the floor. They are both breathing heavily.)

TAMARA: I'm ready now.

MARTIN: We got you where you need to be?

TAMARA: We did.

MARTIN: Fantastic. Let's do it.

TAMARA: I thought today we could focus on playfulness and test out some new locales for lovemaking. You know how after creative foreplay we usually go right into the bedroom?

MARTIN: Yes. Can we just do it, Tam, without the discussion?

TAMARA: *(ignoring him)* What if today we were to clear off the table and... *(She slaps the table hard.)* I feel like this could be a strong and supportive surface for some of our favorite positions.

MARTIN: *(on the verge of impatience)* Agreed! Let's do it.

TAMARA: Do you think it could support The Dragon though?

MARTIN: Yes! I think The Dragon would be dynamite up there! Let's do it!

TAMARA: Wonderful! Let's do it then! I think we'll both enjoy this! *(Beat.)* Well? Aren't you going to help me?

MARTIN: Yes. Fine. Ok.

(In one swift motion he takes a plate from the table and smashes it to the floor.)

MARTIN: Ahhhhhhhhhhhhhh!

(Silence. Even Martin looks surprised.)

TAMARA: Martin!

MARTIN: I'm sorry I— Gosh, I guess... I thought we were being wild?

TAMARA: We weren't! We were not! Go get the dustpan and broom.

MARTIN: Now?

TAMARA: Yes.

MARTIN: But Tam—

TAMARA: Martin? I will not be able to concentrate on pleasuring you if there are shards of plate on the floor. Could we conduct ourselves with some amount of refinement please? Is that possible?

(She hands him the stack of plates.)

MARTIN: Of course. Just a second.

(Martin runs out of the room with the plates. He runs back on with a dustpan and broom, speedily sweeps, and runs back off with the shards. Tamara bolts across the room, snatches a book off the shelf, flips it open and starts reading. Martin runs back on and mounts the table. Beat.)

MARTIN: Uh— Tam? Tammy?

TAMARA: Don't worry, I've forgiven you.

MARTIN: Thank you. Um. Are you reading?

TAMARA: No, just skimming.

MARTIN: Are you... coming back?

(He slaps the table just like Tamara did.)

TAMARA: *(nose in book)* Yes, Beatrice and I just thought of a passage we wanted to recite to you.

MARTIN: That's one of your books though, isn't it?

(She holds up the book.)

TAMARA: Yes, "Pleasure Without Measure: Unearthing Your Clitoral Treasure."

MARTIN: Right, so shouldn't you know what's in there if you wrote it?

TAMARA: Of course!

MARTIN: Well then, please put the book down—

59

TAMARA: I just remember liking the exact way I phrased something.

MARTIN: Tam, please—

TAMARA: This is important, I want to whisper it in your ear during climax.

MARTIN: I DON'T NEED YOU TO RECITE PASSAGES TO ME DURING CLIMAX! THE FACT THAT I'M CLIMAXING IS CLIMAX ENOUGH!!!!

(Beat.)

TAMARA: What was that?!

MARTIN: I'm sorry Tam—

TAMARA: Was that impatience in your tone?

MARTIN: *(calmly)* No. It wasn't. I just think it would be nice if we... improvised. A little. Sometimes. If that's ok with you.

TAMARA: No, it's not ok with me Martin! Improvisation is for people who don't know what they're doing! You know what? Forgive me for trying to plan something special for us. Forgive me for caring so deeply about our sex life that I've mapped out exciting new terrain for us to tackle today...

MARTIN: Tam, the table is exciting terrain. Thank you for suggesting it.

TAMARA: And forgive me for wanting to recite an erotic passage to you that I really think would blow your mind and titillate your senses.

MARTIN: Again, thank you sweetheart. I can't wait to hear it. I'm sorry if I made you think otherwise. *(Beat.)* Forgive me?

(Beat.)

TAMARA: Forgive you. For the plate and for your tone.

MARTIN: Wonderful.

(Beat.)

TAMARA: Well, are we getting up on the table or aren't we?

MARTIN: May as well. Let's do it.

TAMARA: Yes, lets.

(Martin helps her atop of the table.)

MARTIN: Ready to try again?

TAMARA: I am. Happy Sexy Saturday my love.

MARTIN: Happy... "Sexy" Saturday.

(Beat.)

TAMARA: 3... 2... 1!

(Tamara and Beatrice slam on top of him.)

SCENE 7

(Belinda sits in another sparsely decorated apartment. There is a string of hot-chili-pepper-shaped party lights hanging across the wall. She is dressed much more provocatively than before and is wearing bright red lipstick.)

BELINDA: You can do this. Just pretend you're Kathleen Turner in "Body Heat."

(The doorbell rings. Belinda bolts to her feet and grabs her baseball bat.)

MARTIN: *(a loud whisper from offstage)* Belinda?

BELINDA: Yes?

MARTIN: Hi. It's me.

BELINDA: Me? I don't know a "me."

MARTIN: Oh. Right. *(he clears his throat)* Marmoset.

(She throws the bat out of sight, flings the door open, runs to the center of the room and "poses." Martin enters and gently closes the door.)

MARTIN: Wow. Hi.

BELINDA: Hi.

MARTIN: You look—

BELINDA: *(in full "sexy voice")* So do you.

MARTIN: Are those chili peppers? Boy you really—

BELINDA: Shhh. Don't speak.

(She suddenly sprints to him and drops down to her knees. She looks his crotch in the "eye" with full seriousness and starts doing jaw warm-ups and vocalizations.)

MARTIN: Belinda, what are you doing?

BELINDA: *(still in "sexy voice")* Warming up. We are here to have a tawdry, extra-marital affair, are we not?

MARTIN: Well... we may be. I just— Um. Maybe we could... talk first?

(Belinda bolts to her feet.)

BELINDA: WHY CAN'T I READ PEOPLE????

MARTIN: Shhhh, shhhhh. It's ok. Everything fine...

BELINDA: No it's not! I feel so incredibly rude! I'm sorry Martin, I feel skanky, humiliated and lewd! I thought we were both here for sex! Forget I said anything, let's go get some food!

MARTIN: You're speaking in verse!

BELINDA: Yes. I do that sometimes when I'm nervous. Or turned-on. Right now I'm both, so brace yourself, I'm sure more is on the way.

MARTIN: I'm glad to hear it.

BELINDA: That I'm turned on?

MARTIN: That there's more poetry on the way. You're very talented.

BELINDA: Thank you.

(Beat.)

MARTIN: I'm sorry if I'm being confusing. You're lovely. I'm just feeling...

BELINDA: Conflicted?

MARTIN: Yeah.

BELINDA: Gotcha.

(Beat. She bolts to the couch.)

BELINDA: Oooh, stomach and legs, stomach and legs, stomach and legs.

MARTIN: Excuse me?

BELINDA: Stomach and Legs. My very sexual friend told me once that if you're ever trying NOT to be attracted to someone, just imagine that they only have a stomach and legs. Nothing in between. Like a Ken doll. That doesn't exactly help me though right now, to picture Ken, because I'm absolutely attracted to him. If you ask me, the people at Mattel are somewhat irresponsible.

MARTIN: How so?

BELINDA: Well, they purposely manufacture Ken to look like some Greek god, right? They want you to want him. So there you are, a little girl, completely smitten with Ken, and when you finally get brave enough to take his clothes off, you find they've only given him this flesh-colored, slightly bulging mound, outlined to look like underwear. But it doesn't look like underwear. It just looks like disappointment. And you can't even take it off. It's like— glued to him. *(Beat.)* Why are you laughing?

(He sits down beside her.)

MARTIN: You are so funny, you really are.

BELINDA: Yeah, I get that a lot. People usually find me hilarious when I'm trying to be serious.

MARTIN: I'm sorry. It's just... you're adorable.

(He moves closer to her.)

BELINDA: Oh.

MARTIN: That's what I meant to say. That's why I laughed.

BELINDA: Oh.

(She moves closer to him. Beat. They almost kiss.)

MARTIN: I've never cheated on my wife before.

BELINDA: Well I've never done "it" before.

MARTIN: "It"?

BELINDA: "It." You know. The sex.

MARTIN: The sex? You've never had the sex before?

BELINDA: Nope.

MARTIN: Wow.

(Beat.)

BELINDA: Is that a problem?

MARTIN: No it's not a problem, it's just— *(He stares.)* Wow.

BELINDA: Yeah. 35-year old virgin, right here. *(She makes a "raise the roof" gesture.)* Holla back one time.

(Beat. Martin keeps staring.)

BELINDA: No seriously Martin, holla back one time for me. It would break the awkwardness of this moment.

MARTIN: Oh, sure! Uh— *(He raises the roof weakly.)* Holla!

BELINDA: Thank you.

MARTIN: Listen Belinda—

BELINDA: Can you call me Lindy?

MARTIN: Lindy?

BELINDA: Yeah, my friends call me Lindy. .

MARTIN: Alright. I can do that. *(Beat.)* Listen. I don't think we should do this. This seems like a big deal for you and I—

BELINDA: No it's not a big deal at all! I just want to get it over with!

MARTIN: Um.

BELINDA: I'm sorry I didn't mean it like that. I just—
You're so sweet and sexy and I know that you have...
roommates — so we could just, well from what I've
heard it's called a "one-and-done?" We could do that.

MARTIN: You think I'm sexy?

(Beat.)

BELINDA: Beyond sexy, yes.

MARTIN: Really?

BELINDA: Beyond.

(They get very close.)

BELINDA: Oh your minty face drives me totally crazy.
One smell of your face and everything goes hazy. You
make me hotter than films that star Patrick Swayze.

MARTIN: Nervous?

BELINDA: Yeah.

MARTIN: Me too. *(Beat.)* One and done, Lindy?

BELINDA: One and done.

(They kiss.)

SCENE 8

(Two weeks later. Thursday, 3:15pm. Ben is in Belinda's classroom, in the midst of playing Vivaldi's "Autumn" on his violin. It's manic. Fast. Harsh. Strange. Belinda listens. She winces. She works hard to control her face and keep it pleasant. Ben finishes and bows.)

BELINDA: *(relieved)* Oh god, it's over? *(Beat.)* I mean – *(applauding)* WOW! Ben! That was... SOMETHING! What an honor to be serenaded by such a-a-a-a gosh, just a really rigorous musician! Thank you!

BEN: Was it allegro enough?

BELINDA: Was it what?

BEN: Allegro. Enough. That movement I just played was supposed to be allegro.

BELINDA: Allegro means... violent? I'm guessing?

BEN: No. Webster's New World Dictionary defines it as: "Quick. A brisk, lively manner."

BELINDA: Well then, yeah! Yeah, that was quick! And brisk! And... *(under her breath)* scary.

BEN: Excellent. Thank you for your feedback Belinda.

(Ben puts away his violin.)

BELINDA: Hey Ben. Come here. Sit with me.

(Ben sits.)

BELINDA: Let me ask you something. Do you like playing the violin? Is it fun for you?

BEN: Fun?

BELINDA: Yeah, fun.

BEN: Learning how to play an instrument helps my brain cells grow.

BELINDA: That's neat Ben, but—

BEN: It teaches me the merits of discipline and practice. Without discipline and practice, success is unattainable.

BELINDA: Ben? I didn't ask you about discipline or brain cells. I asked if you like playing the violin.

(Beat.)

BEN: No. It hurts my neck.

BELINDA: Hm. So, tell me, what do you like to do?

(Beat.)

BEN: I like to bang things.

BELINDA: That sounds fun. What kinds of things?

BEN: Loud things.

BELINDA: Like...

BEN: Um.

BELINDA: Go ahead.

BEN: Well, our trashcan outside sounds really cool when you drop the recyclables into it and then bang the lid on top. So I do that whenever I can. And, and, and—sometimes I take my thermos and I run it back and forth on the bars of my little sister's crib? That makes a really cool sound like "Uggadah-uggadah-uggadah." Oh, and, and, and— my briefcase sounds really neat when you open it and close it? 'Cause it squeaks a little, but it also makes this funny slappy sound when it shuts and all the air rushes out like "eeeeoooo" and—

BELINDA: Hey Ben?

BEN: Yes?

BELINDA: You sound like a percussionist.

BEN: I do?

BELINDA: You do. *(Beat.)* Listen, your daddy called and said he's going to be late picking you up this after-noon. What do you say we bang some things until he shows up?

BEN: Really?

BELINDA: Sure!

BEN: Ok!

BELINDA: Oh this will be so much fun! Let's look around the classroom and gather things that make great sounds!

BEN: Ok!

(Ben and Belinda run in opposite directions, grabbing blocks, spoons, heavy books, small chairs... whatever they can use to make noise. They toss everything into a pile on the floor. Ben stops.)

BEN: Belinda?

BELINDA: Yeah Ben?

BEN: You're fun.

(Beat.)

BELINDA: Thanks Ben! You're fun too sweetie. *(Beat.)* Ready?

BEN: Ready!

(Belinda looks at Ben and starts tapping a simple rhythm on a table top. She gestures that he should add to it. He hesitates a moment. She encourages him again. He starts slowly rocking a small chair side to side in rhythm.)

BELINDA: Good Ben, that's good. Keep going.

(Ben builds the rocking of the chair until he decides to pick it up and pound it rhythmically and loudly on the floor.)

BELINDA: Great Benny, great! What else do you feel like doing?

(Ben starts adding vocalizations, grunts, yells, whatever he feels like. He and Belinda are really grooving now.)

BELINDA: Wonderful!

(The rhythm builds, until Ben is completely and happily losing his mind, running around the classroom, banging radiators, clapping his hands, laughing, yelling, dancing, all in a great rhythm. Unnoticed by Belinda or Ben, Martin enters and stands in the doorway. He has Beatrice strapped to his chest. She is huge now and takes up most of his body. They are both bundled up in winter coats and hats. They watch the "performance.")

BELINDA: Really go for it Benny!

BEN: I'm going for it!

BELINDA: Yeah you are!

BEN: You like it?

BELINDA: I love it!

BEN: You like it?!?

BELINDA: I love it! Bang the hell outta that thing sweetheart!!!

(Ben and Belinda reach a crescendo of banging. Ben notices Martin first while Belinda continues bang.)

BEN: Hi Daddy!

MARTIN: Hey bud!

(Belinda freezes happily upon hearing his voice, gathers herself and turns to face him.)

BELINDA: *(sexy voice)* Hello Daddy! *(dropping the voice when she sees Bea)* Oh, wow, she's HUGE! I mean — you brought Beatrice!

MARTIN: Yeah. Tamara had a book signing, so...

BEN: Daddy! Belinda and I were banging and banging and banging!

MARTIN: I saw.

BEN: I'm a percussionist!

MARTIN: That's neat Ben. You've got a lot of talent kiddo.

(Martin has unbundled Beatrice, revealing her huge, frightening features and her tangled red hair. Her branches sweep the floor now. Belinda is visibly startled.)

BELINDA: Holy shit!!

BEN: Belinda, you said—

BELINDA: I know Ben, I'm sorry— Your sister is just so... And look at all that... wow. She's really... neat-looking. Beautiful, I mean!

MARTIN: Thank you. We think so.

(Beat. Martin hands Ben a dollar bill.)

MARTIN: *(reluctantly)* Here ya go buddy. Go get your "secret soda."

BEN: Shhhh. It's a seeeeeecret.

MARTIN: *(a bit sadly)* Yeah buddy. Shhhhhh. Kiss?

BEN: Kiss.

(Martin and Ben quickly kiss. Ben pauses a moment.)

BEN: *(to Belinda)* Kiss?

(Beat.)

BELINDA: Kiss.

(Ben and Belinda quickly kiss.)

BEN: Shhhhhh.

BELINDA: Shhhhhh.

(Ben gleefully exits with his dollar. Martin watches him go. Belinda runs right up to Martin, but stops short when she realizes she's about to smack into Beatrice.)

MARTIN: Belinda, wait.

BEATRICE: Can't you... take her off?

MARTIN: No. She can't be without nurturing touch.

BELINDA: Ah. OK. Neither can I.

(She moves in for a kiss, but Martin holds her gently by the shoulders to keep her away.)

MARTIN: Listen—

BELINDA: *(playful, a la "Dirty Dancing")* "Look, spaghetti arms. This is my dance space. This is your dance space. You gotta hold the frame—"

MARTIN: Belinda, stop it with the movie stuff.

BELINDA: *(sexy voice)* Why are you so cold today, hot stuff?

MARTIN: I'm not, I just—

BELINDA: Alright, you're not. *(sexy voice)* So...I have a new listing in Bed Stuy for this Saturday night, aka, our threeeee week anniversary. Nice hardwood floors. *(quick beat)* Well, sort of. I'll Swiffer before you get there, hot stuff.

MARTIN: No need.

BELINDA: *(still in sexy voice)* No, really. It's Bed Stuy. Gotta swiffer.

MARTIN: Belinda, I've been thinking.

BELINDA: No no. Don't think. Don't think. Don't think.

(She goes in for another kiss. He holds her off again.)

MARTIN: It's Ben—

BELINDA: *(startled, looking around)* Where's Ben?

MARTIN: No, Ben's been acting strange. I think he's picking up on—

75

BELINDA: Relax, we have at least a minute before Ben gets back.

MARTIN: I'm speaking here, ok? Will you listen to me?

BELINDA: This isn't "speaking" time. This is "Ben's going to be back from his 'secret soda' in two seconds and I won't see you again til Saturday night time!"

MARTIN: It's over Lindy.

BELINDA: Nope.

MARTIN: I'm never leaving my wife. I'm never leaving Ben.

BELINDA: Well, eventually you will...

MARTIN: *(firm)* No. Never. This was a mistake.

(Ben re-enters unseen, drinking a Dr. Pepper.)

MARTIN: We said one and done, and it's been several now and—

BELINDA: Three to be exact. Don't you think I'm improving? I thought last time at the Cobble Hill walk-up was really dynamite—

MARTIN: It's just starting to feel like we're having an affair at this point—

BELINDA: Well?? We are!

(She forcibly takes his hands and plants them on her breasts.)

BEN: Daddy, you're touching Belinda's boobies.

MARTIN: No I'm not.

(Martin's hands drop. Silence.)

BEN: Daddy?

(Beat.)

MARTIN: Yeah bud?

BEN: What's an affair?

MARTIN: It's uh— a fancy party, pal.

BEN: Oh. And you and Belinda had one?

MARTIN: No, we did not.

BELINDA: Actually Ben... yes. Yes we did.

MARTIN: No, we did not. Belinda??

BEN: I love parties! Did you play pin the tail on the donkey??

BELINDA: Why yes Ben, we did! In a really nice studio in Ditmas Park!

MARTIN: Ben? Get your things. We're leaving.

BEN: Why didn't you invite meeeee to Ditmas Park?

MARTIN: Ben. There was no party in Ditmas Park. Belinda's being silly.

BEN: That's too bad. Parties are fun.

BELINDA: They sure are. And your Daddy throws a hell of a good one!

MARTIN: No I don't. Parties are very very bad Ben. Let's go.

BELINDA: Martin, don't go. I'm sorry! *(singing)* "Don't go changin..."

MARTIN: I'm sorry, Belinda, we're going.

BELINDA: *(singing)* "...to try and please me..."

BEN: But I'm not done my secret soda yet!

(Martin takes the soda out of his hand and throws it in the trash.)

MARTIN: We're done with secret soda.

BELINDA: *(singing)* "...Don't change the color of your hair..."

BEN: But Daddy, we're not doing our part. We need to recycle! Why is Belinda singing?

MARTIN: Ben, enough!

(Martin drags Ben toward the door by the arm.)

BEN: Ow, Daddy!

BELINDA: I— "gave you my heart, you gave me your pen!!!"

BEN: Belinda, you can borrow my pen!

BELINDA: I-I-I- "carried a watermelon!"

BEN: I can carry your watermelon!

MARTIN: Enough Belinda!

BELINDA: Martin! If you leave right now, I'll— I'll— "Boil your bunny!" Please don't go—

(The door slams. A moment of silence.)

BELINDA: I'll boil your bunny.

SCENE 9

(Same day, 5:00pm. Tamara's dining room. Ben is at his music stand, violin on shoulder, bow raised as if he's going to play. But he doesn't. He just stares blankly into space.)

TAMARA: Ben?

(No answer.)

TAMARA: Benjamin, we're very excited for our concert. Yay!

(She attempts to "clap" Bea's branches.)

TAMARA: Benny?

BEN: Mommy? Have you ever boiled a bunny?

TAMARA: Have I ever boiled a bunny. Can't say that I have, angel. Though bunnies are Paleo friendly! I don't think they sell bunnies at our grocery store. I bet if we took a trip to one of those grassy places outside of the city where people shoot things we could find some. Would you like that?

BEN: Maybe.

TAMARA: Well we'll have to do that sometime then. Now, come help Mommy get dinner. Daddy will be back in a few minutes and we'll eat our gazpacho.

BEN: Daddy's in a bad mood today.

TAMARA: Why do you say that Ben?

BEN: He just is.

TAMARA: Hm. Hadn't noticed. Well, bad moods are a choice, so Daddy will just have to choose differently. Mommy always chooses good moods. That's why she's always so much fun to be around.

(Martin walks in and drops a bag on the counter. He is overly cheery.)

MARTIN: A quarter cup of carob powder, one tablespoon of raw honey, 4 almost-brown bananas, and 8 loose prunes!

TAMARA: Mmmm. What a yummy dessert we're going to have!

MARTIN: Can't wait.

BEN: Daddy. Mommy and I were just discussing your bad mood and how you should make better choices.

MARTIN: Fantastic buddy. How bout we disrobe.

BEN: Fine.

(They disrobe and fold. Ben eyes Martin sternly. Tamara watches this in confusion. Ben slowly takes the clothes to the family hamper, never taking his eyes off Martin.)

TAMARA: Martin. What's this I hear about a "bad mood?"

MARTIN: Huh?

TAMARA: Your son says you're in a "bad" mood.

MARTIN: But I'm never in a bad mood. "Bad moods are a choice and—"

TAMARA AND MARTIN: "Our family always chooses good moods."

TAMARA: I know, that's why I found his comment puzzling.

MARTIN: Huh.

(Ben returns.)

MARTIN: Welcome back buddy!

(Ben is silent. He glares at Martin.)

TAMARA: Benjamin?

BEN: Yes Mommy?

TAMARA: Ready for our invocation?

BEN: Yes Mommy.

(They all join hands.)

TAMARA, MARTIN, BEN: "Dear Universal Energy, we invoke you now to bless this food. May it nourish our very attractive bodies. May you—"

MARTIN: You know what guys?

(Tamara and Ben stop invoking. Beat.)

MARTIN: Let's try something different tonight.

TAMARA: Excuse me?

MARTIN: Hey Benny, wanna try something fun?

TAMARA: Martin, what are you doing?

MARTIN: *(to Ben)* What do you say we create a new invocation. As a family. Everyone gets a say.

BEN: Even me?

MARTIN: Especially you buddy. Let's sit down.

TAMARA: But Martin—

MARTIN: Sit down!

(They all sit.)

MARTIN: Ben, you give us a beat, and—

(Ben looks to Tamara.)

MARTIN: Go ahead pal, give us a beat.

(Ben starts tapping the table.)

MARTIN: Great. Now we'll go around the table and word by word we'll create our invocation for the evening.

TAMARA: Martin, this is—

MARTIN: Fun, Tam. This is fun. I'll start. *(Beat.)* "Dear...

(Beat. He points to Tamara. She is struggling.)

TAMARA: ...Universal

BEN: ...Energy!!!"

MARTIN: Good! "Bless...

TAMARA: ...This

BEN: Gazpacho!!!!!!!"

MARTIN: Beautiful! How bout a drum solo Ben?

BEN: Oh! Totally!!!

(Ben wails on the table.)

MARTIN: Fantastic. Let's keep going. "May...

TAMARA: ...this food...

BEN: ...be tasty and delicious and may there be leftovers that I can have for a snack tomorrow!!!!!!!!"

(Ben wails on the table even more.)

MARTIN: Brilliant kiddo. "Thank you...

TAMARA: ...for

BEN: ...Ben!!!!!"

MARTIN: Absolutely! "Thank you for Ben and....

TAMARA: ...Beatrice...

BEN: And Mommy and Daddy and Belinda!!!

MARTIN: Belinda?

BEN: Yeah!!!!!!!! Thank you for Belinda!!!!!

TAMARA: His teacher sweetheart, he's grateful for his teacher.

(Silence.)

MARTIN: This was fun guys. Let's eat.

(They all dive into their soup. It's quiet for a few moments.)

TAMARA: I actual received a phone call from Belinda this afternoon.

(Martin spits his gazpacho.)

BEN: Daddy, you spit your gazpacho.

MARTIN: Who?

TAMARA: Ben's teacher? Really Martin, you should know her name by now. You see this woman everyday.

BEN: Yeah Daddy! She likes you. And you like her. Sometimes you even touch her boo—

MARTIN: Yeah, sport! Of course I know your teacher's name. I'm just— Why were you on the phone with her, Tam? Was there another problem at school?

(Beat.)

85

TAMARA: No, quite the opposite actually. She called to apologize.

(Beat.)

MARTIN: For what?

TAMARA: For contaminating Ben with grains and bovine milk. Apparently she's been feeling quite guilty about it.

MARTIN: Ah.

TAMARA: We talked for quite a while! It was delightful actually.

BEN: Mommy and Belinda share everything. They're best friends!

MARTIN: No they're not buddy.

TAMARA: No, it's true. She and I have decided to be great friends.

(Beat.)

MARTIN: But you hate having friends.

TAMARA: I know! Especially female friends! It's usually such a hassle pretending to care about their feelings and their problems, so I'd just as soon do without. But Belinda doesn't seem to have any feelings, which is refreshing. And her obvious problems make me feel even more accomplished than I usually do. I can't wait to see her tomorrow.

MARTIN: What's tomorrow?

TAMARA: Belinda's invited me to come in early tomorrow morning to drop off Ben and have tea with her. Isn't that sweet?

MARTIN: But I always drop Ben off.

TAMARA: Not tomorrow. Oh, I'm excited. I'm not used to people inviting me to visit them. I usually show up by force. This is a nice change.

MARTIN: Did she say why?

TAMARA: "Girl chat." That's how she said it. "Girl Chat."

BEN: "Girl chat."

TAMARA: Isn't that just adorable?

MARTIN: "Girl Chat."

BEN: "Girl Chat."

(They all have a hearty laugh.)

MARTIN: I'm coming with you.

TAMARA: Sweetheart, you weren't invited.

MARTIN: I'm coming with you.

SCENE 10

(7:30am Brooklyn Independent Learning School. Belinda's classroom. Belinda is sitting in a small chair and staring at the door. She has makeup on. She is dressed way too sexy to be teaching kindergarten, with a low cut top and very short skirt. The door flies open and Ben bypasses Belinda, heading right to the cubby area.)

BELINDA: Hey Benny boy!

(Ben looks at her a moment, then settles down and starts working.)

BELINDA: Ben? *(Beat.)* Ben, where's your Mommy?

(Tamara enters.)

TAMARA: Well look at you, Lindy!

BELINDA: No, look at YOU, Tammy!

(Tamara licks her thumb and zooms it close to Belinda's face.)

TAMARA: Oh, you have something— *(She looks closer.)* Ah, it's a blemish. Forgive me, when you're a mother you're always at the ready with a wet thumb.

(Martin enters unnoticed. He is wearing Bea. He watches the two women.)

BELINDA: That's fine! Thank you for caring enough to lick your thumb for me.

TAMARA: You bet Lindy.

(Tamara opens her arms and they embrace like old girl-friends, holding too long and swaying side to side.)

TAMARA: Mmmmm. Hugs are good.

BELINDA: They sure are.

MARTIN: Hello Miss Cartwright.

(The women break their hug.)

BELINDA: I wasn't expecting you to join us Mr. Laurence.

MARTIN: I know you weren't.

BELINDA: Your wife and I are just having some—

MARTIN: "Girl Chat." Yes, I heard. Sounds fun.

BELINDA: I'm afraid you'll be rather bored.

MARTIN: That's fine.

TAMARA: I tried to tell him that but, I suppose he felt left out knowing the rest of the family would be here. My Martin is such a family man.

BELINDA: So he seems. You're very lucky.

(Tamara stares at Belinda's breasts.)

TAMARA: Yes I am. Lindy, I have to say, I'm a bit distracted by your—

BELINDA: Physique?

TAMARA: Yes! But pleasantly so! Last time we met you were so soft and spiritless, rather cheese-like. But today! Today you look robust! I like it. A bit inappropriate for teaching kindergarten, but still, I like it!

BELINDA: Thank you very much Tammy! *(gesturing to the table)* Shall we?

TAMARA: Oh yes, let's.

(The three adults sit down at the tiny table.)

TAMARA: Oh this is delightful! Such a sweet little tea party!

BEN: Mommy, Daddy and Belinda didn't have a fancy party.

(Beat.)

TAMARA: Well of course they didn't, love. Why would Daddy and Belinda have a fancy party?

BEN: They wouldn't. *(Beat.)* They didn't play pin the tail on the donkey or give me secret sodas either.

TAMARA: What? You are being such a silly boy today, Ben. This is one of the many reasons you need to procreate, Belinda. Not only do these precious creatures add tremendous value to your life, but they keep you laughing with all the charming things they say.

BEN: I'm charming.

TAMARA: You certainly are.

MARTIN: Ben, your inferior classmates will be here soon. Go get to work, ok pal?

BEN: No Daddy.

MARTIN: Benjamin?

BEN: Daddy?

MARTIN: Benjamin?

BEN: Daddy?

MARTIN: Benjamin?

BEN: Daddy?

MARTIN: Ben, GO!!!!!!!!!!!

(Ben stares at Martin a moment, then walks over to a work station, takes out a stuffed puppy and starts handling it roughly.)

TAMARA: Martin, what on earth has gotten into you?

BELINDA: I think I can answer that question Tammy. I actually know quite a bit about what Martin's been "getting into" lately. That's the real reason I asked you to come in today. You should know that—

(Tamara's attention has turned to the corner where Ben is abusing the stuffed puppy.)

TAMARA: Belinda, I'm going to need you to shut up for a moment.

(Beat. Ben is breastfeeding the puppy.)

TAMARA: Martin. Look at Benjamin. Does he seem disturbed to you?

BELINDA: Absolutely.

TAMARA: Belinda, I didn't ask you. Martin?

(Ben is humping the puppy. A beat as they all watch.)

MARTIN: No. He seems...fine.

TAMARA: I wonder if he's not getting enough of our attention now that Baby Bea is here.

(Ben has collapsed into a fetal position.)

TAMARA: Yes, that's it. He's silently yet desperately calling out for us. Belinda, I need to ask for your assistance with something.

BELINDA: What's that?

TAMARA: I need you to wear our daughter.

BELINDA: Oh— god— I—

TAMARA: Yes. This will be a nice moment for us all. Let's bond. Ben needs his mother and father right now, and we obviously can't allow Beatrice to be without nurturing touch for even a moment.

MARTIN: Tam— I can keep her—

TAMARA: Martin, no. *(to Belinda)* Can I trust you to wear our daughter and offer her appropriate tactile sensations while we communicate love to our son?

MARTIN: Tamara, let's just go home and communicate love to him there—

TAMARA: Martin, no! We will communicate love to him right this very second! Belinda?

BELINDA: Uhhh.... Yes. You can trust me to... wear and sensitize your daughter.

TAMARA: Excellent. Belinda, stand up and look Beatrice in the eye.

(Belinda walks over to Martin looks him right in the eye. He stares back.)

TAMARA: No, not Martin! Beatrice!

(Belinda squats down to get on eye level with Bea.)

TAMARA: Wonderful. You've completed the first step in infant communication. Now, I need you to establish physical contact with her before I can hand her to you.

(Belinda touches Bea with her index finger only.)

TAMARA: That will never do. Heart to heart please. *(Beat.)* Heart to heart!

(Tamara smooshes Belinda and Martin together. They awkwardly negotiate the transfer until Belinda is wearing Beatrice.)

BELINDA: Well hello there, you... sweet little pumpkin, you!

TAMARA: Don't talk down to her. She'll end you. *(Beat.)* Benjamin? *(Beat.)* Benjamin, Mommy is talking to you.

(Beat.)

TAMARA: *(in desperation)* Benjamin, put down the puppy)!

(He does. Tamara lowers herself on to her knees and reaches her arms out to him.)

TAMARA: Come here baby!

(Ben runs into her arms and they hug fiercely.)

TAMARA: Mommy's so sorry!

BEN: I love you Mommy!

TAMARA: I love you too sweetheart! Have you been a sad boy because Mommy's spending so much time with your little sister?

(He nods.)

TAMARA: Would some family lap time make you feel better?

(He nods.)

TAMARA: It's decided then. Come here angel.

(Martin looks lost.)

TAMARA: Martin! I need you awake! *(She snaps.)* Alert! *(She snaps.)* Alive! *(She snaps.)*

MARTIN: Tam, we're not really going to do this here, are we?

TAMARA: Of course we are. Please get into position for family lap time.

MARTIN: Lap time can wait until we get home—

BEN: I NEED FAMILY LAP TIME NOW!!!!!!!!!!

MARTIN: Alright, alright!

(Martin gets into position. Tamara sits on his lap. Ben sits on Tamara's lap)

TAMARA: And... begin.

(Ben immediately starts batting at Tamara's breasts, tugging at them, tossing them side to side etc. Martin massages Tamara's shoulders and begins the family mantra. He continues mantra-ing underneath Tamara and Belinda's next exchange. Belinda watches in horror.)

MARTIN: "We are powerful, we are delightful, we are the Jenkins-Laurence Family.... We are powerful, we are delightful, we are the Jenkins-Laurence Family... "

TAMARA: Mmmmmmm. Good job boys. Belinda, it's not going to bother you if Ben and Martin explore my body for a bit, is it?

BELINDA: Uh... No. No, why would it? That's a-a-beautiful, natural thing happening over there.

TAMARA: It is. Please, pull up a chair and join us.

BELINDA: I'll stand, thank you.

(The "boys" continue to rub and explore.)

TAMARA: Well, look at you Belinda! You look much better with a baby strapped to you! Alright, now let's try to forget the boys are here and get back to our "girl chat." I'm assuming you need sex advice?

BELINDA: Sex advice? No. Why would you assume that?

TAMARA: Well, I've been watching you very closely...

BELINDA: And...?

TAMARA: Despite your efforts with the push-up bra, which I commend you for, you're still quite sexless. It's clear that you need to have more intercourse. Are you currently copulating?

(Martin abruptly stops chanting. Silence.)

TAMARA: Martin, please continue.

BEN: Yes, Daddy, please continue!

MARTIN: Oh my god, "We are powerful, we are delightful, we are the Jenkins-Laurence family...

TAMARA: *(to Belinda)* So? Are you? I'm proud to say that Martin and I copulate once a week.

BELINDA: That's fantastic, so do we we!

(Martin's chanting gets extremely loud.)

TAMARA: *(competing with the noise)* I'm sorry, what?

BELINDA: I said— that's fantastic, that's very sweet!

TAMARA: Yes, it is. It's very satisfying. *(looking at her watch)* Alright boys, it's time we wrapped things up. And...3...2...1... Finish. *(to Ben)* Kiss?

BEN: Kiss.

(Ben and Tamara quickly kiss.)

TAMARA: *(to Martin)* Kiss?

MARTIN: Kiss.

(Tamara and Martin quickly kiss.)

MARTIN: *(to Ben)* Kiss?

BEN: *(angry)* NO.

(Beat.)

TAMARA: *(confused)* Benjamin... didn't you enjoy playing with Mommy's boobies?

BEN: Yes. Very much.

TAMARA: Oh good. Motherhood is such a gift. Thank you Belinda, I'll take Beatrice back now.

(Family lap time disbands. Tamara places her chest on Bea and starts unbuckling her from Belinda. For a moment the two women are practically mouth to mouth.)

BEN: Mommy, did you notice I tried some new techniques?

TAMARA: I thought there was a new move in there! Very clever, Ben.

BEN: I learned it from watching Daddy and Belinda.

(Tamara freezes and stares at Belinda.)

TAMARA: Watching Daddy and Belinda do what, sweetheart?

MARTIN: Ben?

BEN: Daddy??????!?!

TAMARA: Benjamin, focus on Mommy. Watching Daddy and Belinda do what, angel?

BEN: Lap time. Only they do it standing up. And without the family mantra.

(Silence.)

TAMARA: Martin? Is this true?

MARTIN: Tam—

BELINDA: Yes it is true, Tammy. "It's very satisfying."

MARTIN: Tam—

(Martin rushes to Tamara and tries to touch her. She pushes him away. She looks blankly at Belinda. Silence.)

BELINDA: This is a first. You usually have so much to say. Let me guess. Am I not as "sexless" as you once imagined? Or did you just not expect me to stick my breast into your cow's mouth?

(Beat.)

BELINDA: Holla!!!

(Silence.)

(Tamara moves slowly upstage and hands Beatrice to Ben. Then she turns and leaps on Belinda like a savage monkey. They scream. They pull hair. They roll and fight. Martin dives in to break up the fray and takes a few blows and hair pulls himself. Ben watches. After some struggle, Martin manages to split the women up and hold them apart from one another. All three adults take a large collective breath and then launch into a simultaneous explosion of words. Note: the following 3 short speeches start and end at exactly the same time, over-lapping completely.)

MARTIN: TAMARA CAN'T WE TALK ABOUT THIS?! BELINDA, WHAT THE HELL HAPPENED TO YOU, YOU WERE SO SWEET! TAMARA I'M SORRY I JUST WANTED A REAL GODDAMN SEX LIFE THAT DIDN'T INVOLVE A MANUAL AND A STOP WATCH! OR AN INFANT FOR THAT MATTER! OH FUCK TONY ROBBINS! BELINDA GET LOST! GO WATCH GOONIES AND LEAVE MY FAMILY THE HELL ALONE!

TAMARA: I DO NOT GET HUMILIATED LIKE THIS! NO MARTIN, WE CANNOT TALK ABOUT THIS! I DO NOT GET DISRESPECTED, THIS ISN'T HOW MY LIFE WORKS! SECRET SODA??? WHAT KIND? WHAT KIND?! TONY ROBBINS USES A MANUAL AND A STOP WATCH AND IT WORKS FOR HIM JUST FINE! DR. PEPPER?? I'D LOVE TO FUCK TONY ROBBINS MARTIN, THANK YOU!

BELINDA: HOW CAN YOU LET HER TREAT ME LIKE THIS? GUESS WHAT TAMARA? I PUMPED YOUR KID FULL OF SECRET SODAS EVERY DAY! SORRY MARTIN, SWEETNESS GOES SOUR WHEN IT GETS SPIT ON! YOU SEEM WORKED UP TAMMY, WHAT'S WRONG, TOO MANY CHEERIOS? DOCTOR PEPPER! DOCTOR PEPPER!!! DOCTOR PEPPER!! WHO'S "SOFT AND CHEESE-LIKE" NOW? HUH? HUH?

BEN: Hey!!!!!!!!

(Beat.)

BEN: EVERYBODY DISROBE SO WE CAN CONNECT!!!!!!!

TAMARA: Benjamin, be a good boy and let the grown-ups—

(Ben thrusts Beatrice high above his head.)

BEN: EVERYONE DISROBE RIGHT THIS SECOND OR I'LL THROW MY FREAK OF A BABY SISTER ACROSS THE ROOM!!!!!!

MARTIN: Benny boy, I—

(With a primal growl, Ben lassos Bea overhead, her branches creating a terrifying helicopter of sorts that nearly slices the adults.)

BEN: Rrrrrrrrrrrrrrrrrrrrrrr!

MARTIN, TAMARA, BELINDA: *(collective scream)*

(Silence. Ben holds his sister close. Tamara, Martin and Belinda are crouched on the floor, staring at him helplessly.)

BEN: *(menacing)* Do it.

(They get up slowly and strip down to their undergarments. Tamara and Martin are in their usual dinner attire, Belinda is wearing "days of the week" underpants with a clashing push-up bra.)

TAMARA: Good god, days-of-the-week panties? Are you actually a toddler, Belinda?

BELINDA: Boy, I'm so sorry TaMAra. I wasn't planning on being sexually assaulted by your five-year-old today!

TAMARA: Oh, had you known, you'd have worn your big-girl panties? Is this the kind of woman you want Martin?

(Ben has positioned Beatrice as a backpack and approaches Belinda's waistband. He starts angry-nuzzling Belinda's belly.)

BEN: Rrrrrrrrrrrrrr.

MARTIN: Ben buddy, please get your face away from your teacher's panties.

BELINDA: *(giggling)* Benny, stop!

BEN: *(still nuzzling)* Daddy are you jealous?

TAMARA: Benjamin, that's enough!

BELINDA: *(still giggling)* Benny...

(Ben nuzzles even more.)

BEN: Are you jealous Daddy, are you jealous?

TAMARA: Benjamin, please!

BEN: *(nuzzling)* Rrrrrrrrrrr!

BELINDA: *(still giggling)* Ben!

MARTIN: Ben, Daddy's not kidding now!

BEN: *(nuzzling)* Rrrrrrrrrrrrr!

MARTIN: STOP!!!!

(Martin pushes Ben away from Belinda, hard. Ben stumbles but manages to stay upright and keep Beatrice on his back. Silence.)

TAMARA: Martin, how could you?!! *(Beat.)* Benjamin, baby, let's go home. Daddy and Belinda can go be lecherous together in her ridiculous Tuesday panties while you and I go enjoy a nice coconut-based ice treat together. Ok baby? Hand your sister to Mommy and we'll go have some fun. You and me.

(Beat. Ben glares at Tamara.)

TAMARA: Benny?

(Ben snaps off one of Beatrice's branches and throws it at Tamara.)

MARTIN: *(simultaneous)* Ben, no!

TAMARA: *(simultaneous)* Benjamin!!!

BELINDA: *(simultaneous)* Benjamin, sweetie, you know there's no throwing things in the classroom!

(Ben takes hold of another branch and pauses.)

TAMARA: Ben, leave your sister alone!

BEN: It's ok, Mommy, she doesn't feel anything!

TAMARA: Of course she feels things Benjamin! She's a person!

(Ben considers a moment then breaks off the other three branches and throws them at Martin, Tamara and Belinda. They dodge the flying limbs as Ben lifts Beatrice high in the air.)

MARTIN, TAMARA, BELINDA: BEN, NO!!!!!!!!!!!!!!!

(With one sickening smack, Ben slams Beatrice to the floor. Everyone freezes in horror.)

BEN: I LEARNED IT FROM WATCHING YOU, ALRIGHT???? I LEARNED IT FROM WATCHING YOU!!!!!!!!!!!

(Beat.)

BELINDA: *(quietly)* Is he quoting that very moving anti-drug PSA from the late 80s? Such a powerful campaign.

MARTIN: Belinda, please.

(They all stare at the broken baby. After a moment, Tamara very slowly and silently approaches Beatrice. She gets down on her knees, picks her up, and rocks her. A long beat. Ben starts to cry.)

BEN: Mommy, I'm sorry, I—

TAMARA: Shhhh Ben.

(Beat.)

MARTIN: Tam. Is she—?

TAMARA: Shhhh Martin.

(Beat.)

BELINDA: Should I call—?

TAMARA: I know you don't need me to tell you to—

BELINDA: Shhhhh, yes. Shhh.

(Ben, Belinda and Martin stand separately from one another and a considerable distance away from Tamara and Baby Bea. Tamara continues to rock her in silence. Ben, Belinda and Martin gradually pick up the rocking rhythm in their own bodies. Everyone sways in their separate spaces, all eyes on Bea.)

TAMARA: Shhhhhhhhhhh.

END OF PLAY.